DISCARD

Máquinas maravillosas/Mighty Machines

Tanques/Tanks

por/by Matt Doeden

Traducción/Translation: Martín Luis Guzmán Ferrer, Ph.D.
Editor Consultor/Consulting Editor: Dra. Gail Saunders-Smith

Capstone
press

Mankato, Minnesota

Pebble Plus is published by Capstone Press,
151 Good Counsel Drive, P.O. Box 669, Mankato, Minnesota 56002.
www.capstonepress.com

1 2 3 4 5 6 11 10 09 08 07 06

Library of Congress Cataloging-in-Publication Data
Doeden, Matt.
    [Tanks. Spanish & English]
    Tanques=Tanks/by Matt Doeden.
    p. cm.—(Pebble plus. Máquinas maravillosas=Pebble plus. Mighty machines)
    Includes index.
    ISBN-13: 978-0-7368-5877-9 (hardcover)
    ISBN-10: 0-7368-5877-6 (hardcover)
    1. Tanks (Military science)—Juvenile literature. I. Title. II. Series: Pebble plus. Máquinas maravillosas.
UG446.5.D6218 2005
623.7'4752—dc22   2005019059

Summary: Simple text and photographs present military tanks, their parts, and their crew.

Editorial Credits
Martha E. H. Rustad, editor; Jenny Marks, bilingual editor; Eida del Risco, Spanish copy editor; Molly Nei, set designer; Kate Opseth and Ted Williams, book designer; Jo Miller, photo researcher; Scott Thoms, photo editor

Photo Credits
Corbis/George Hall, 20–21
Digital Vision, 1
DVIC/Chuck Croston, 17; JOSN Gael Rene, 18–19; PH1 (NAC) Stephen Batiz, 14–15; SPC Christina Ann Horne, 13; SPC David Faas, 10–11; Steve Catlin, cover
Fotodynamics/Ted Carlson, 4–5, 6–7, 8–9

Note to Parents and Teachers

The Mighty Machines set supports national standards related to science, technology, and society. This book describes and illustrates tanks. The images support early readers in understanding the text. The repetition of words and phrases helps early readers learn new words. This book also introduces early readers to subject-specific vocabulary words, which are defined in the Glossary section. Early readers may need assistance to read some words and to use the Table of Contents, Glossary, Internet Sites, and Index sections of the book.

Table of Contents

Tabla de contenidos

What Are Tanks?

Tanks are mighty fighting
machines. Armies use tanks
in battles.

¿Qué son los tanques?

Los tanques son poderosas máquinas
para pelear. Los ejércitos
utilizan los tanques en las batallas.

Parts of Tanks

Tanks roll on small wheels.
Long tracks cover the wheels.
Tracks help tanks move
over rough ground.

Las partes de los tanques

Los tanques se mueven sobre ruedas pequeñas que están cubiertas por bandas alargadas. Las bandas sirven para que los tanques puedan moverse en terrenos irregulares.

wheel/rueda

track/bandas

7

Tanks are covered in armor.
This metal shell protects
the crew inside.

Los tanques están cubiertos por
un blindaje. Esta cubierta
de metal protege a la tripulación
que está dentro del tanque.

Tanks have big guns
called cannons. Cannons
can turn in any direction.

Los tanques tiene unas armas enormes
que se llaman cañones. Los cañones
pueden moverse en cualquier dirección.

Tanks have machine guns.
Tank crews fire machine guns
during battles.

Los tanques tienen ametralladoras.
La tripulación dispara con las
ametralladoras durante las batallas.

machine gun/ametralladora

Tank Crews

Commanders are in charge of tanks. They give orders to the rest of the crew.

La tripulación de los tanques

Los comandantes están al mando de los tanques. Ellos dan las órdenes al resto de la tripulación.

Drivers steer tanks.
They sit in the front.

Los conductores guían los tanques.
Ellos se sientan al frente.

driver/conductores

17

Gunners aim at targets.
They fire the guns.

Los artilleros apuntan al blanco.
Ellos disparan las armas.

Mighty Machines

Crews drive tanks into battle.
Tanks are mighty machines.

Máquinas maravillosas

La tripulación conduce los tanques
a las batallas. Los tanques
son unas máquinas maravillosas.

Glossary

aim—to point a weapon at a target

armor—a tank's metal covering; armor protects a tank from bullets and bombs.

army—a group of people trained to fight on land

cannon—a large gun that fires large shells

commander—a person who leads a tank crew

crew—a team of people who work together

gunner—a crew member who shoots a tank's weapons

machine gun—a gun that can fire bullets quickly without reloading

steer—to make a vehicle go in a certain direction

target—an object at which to aim or shoot

track—a piece of metal and rubber that stretches around a tank's wheels

Glosario

ametralladora—arma que puede disparar balas rápidamente sin necesidad de recargarla

apuntar—dirigir una arma al blanco

artillero—miembro de la tripulación que dispara las armas del tanque

banda—pieza de metal y goma que envuelve las ruedas del tanque

blanco—objeto al que se apunta o dispara

blindaje—cubierta de metal del tanque; el blindaje protege a los tanques de las balas y las bombas.

cañón—arma grande que dispara proyectiles

comandante—persona que dirige a la tripulación del tanque

ejército—grupo de personas entrenadas para combatir en tierra

guiar—hacer que un vehículo vaya en cierta dirección

tripulación—grupo de personas que trabaja en equipo

Internet Sites

FactHound offers a safe, fun way to find Internet sites related to this book. All of the sites on FactHound have been researched by our staff.

Here's how:

1) Visit *www.facthound.com*

2) Type in this special code **0736836594** for age-appropriate sites. Or enter a search word related to this book for a more general search.

3) Click on the **FETCH IT** button.

FactHound will fetch the best sites for you!

Sitios de Internet

FactHound te ofrece una manera segura y divertida para encontrar sitios de Internet relacionados con este libro. Todos los sitios de FactHound han sido investigados por nuestro equipo. Es posible que los sitios no estén en español.

Así:

1) Ve a *www.facthound.com*

2) Teclea la clave especial **0736836594** para los sitios apropiados por edad. O teclea una palabra relacionada con este libro para una búsqueda más general.

3) Clic en el botón de **FETCH IT**.

¡FactHound buscará los mejores sitios para ti!